WITH THE WORD

A Bible Study and Devotional Guide
for Groups or Individuals

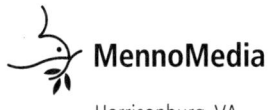

Harrisonburg, VA
Waterloo, ON

With the Word: Isaiah
Copyright © 2012 by MennoMedia, Harrisonburg, Virginia 22802.
  Released simultaneously in Canada by MennoMedia,
  Waterloo, Ontario N2L 6H7. All rights reserved.
International Standard Book Number: 978-0-8361-9641-2
Printed in United States of America.
Edited by Linda Gehman Peachey, cover and interior design by Merrill R. Miller.

Sessions from *Adult Bible Study Teacher* and *Adult Bible Study Student*, along with *Rejoice!* daily devotions, were all used in the writing of *With the Word: Isaiah*.

All rights reserved. This publication may not be reproduced, stored in a retrieval system, or transmitted in whole or in part, in any form, by any means, electronic, mechanical, photocopying, recording or otherwise without prior permission of the copyright owners.

Scripture quotation taken from the Holy Bible, *New Revised Standard Version Bible*, copyright ©1989, Division of Christian Education of the National Council of the Churches of Christ in the United States of America. Used by permission. All rights reserved.

To order or request information, please call 1-800-245-7894 in the U.S. or 1-800-631-6535 in Canada. Or visit www.MennoMedia.org.

15 14 13 12   10 9 8 7 6 5 4 3 2 1

Table of contents

INTRODUCTION
5

SESSION FORMAT
7

1. COMMITMENT TO CHANGE (ISAIAH 6:1-13)
8

2. GOD'S PEOPLE COMFORTED (ISAIAH 40)
14

3. RECREATING COMMUNITY (ISAIAH 43:1-13)
20

4. RESTORATION AND BLESSING (ISAIAH 43:14–44:8)
26

5. STRENGTH FROM GOD (ISAIAH 49:5-6; 50:4-9)
32

6. TRUST GOD (ISAIAH 51:1-16)
38

7. FINDING SATISFACTION (ISAIAH 55:1-11)
44

8. GOOD NEWS (ISAIAH 61)
50

Introduction

❖ ❖

Welcome to *With the Word*! This exciting series from MennoMedia invites you to draw closer to God by spending time with the Word through Bible study and daily devotions.

Studying Isaiah

The focus of attention in the book of Isaiah is concern for a distinct people with a particular relationship to God in the context of imperial interests. The mediating agent in this concern is the larger circle of the Isaiah prophetic tradition.

The concern for a particular people is most clearly stated in the name of *the Lord as the Holy One of Israel*. This name indicates a relationship between *Israel* as people and *the Holy One* as deity. The emphasis on God's holiness in the book of Isaiah arises in the vision of God's exalted greatness on his kingly throne in Isaiah 6:1-4.

The Holy One of Israel may at first glance appear to be concerned only with Israel. The witness of the book of Isaiah, however, yields an altogether different picture. The Lord is not only the God of a particular people but also God of the nations. This overarching theme may be expressed as the Lord's universal kingship or as his monopoly of power over history.

The overall purpose of the book is to show how God's rule among his own people becomes the means by which the nations of the earth receive the blessing promised to Abram in Genesis 12:1-3 and reaffirmed during Abraham's lifetime. And what is that promised blessing? In the first place, the blessing was on Abraham and his family—to become a great nation with a great name. To achieve such greatness, Abraham is charged to "keep the way of the Lord by doing righteousness and justice." In Isaiah the same language is used to indicate the Lord's way for his people.

The blessing was to move through Abraham and his descendants to "all the families of the earth." In the book of Isaiah the swords-to-plowshares text and the Servant Songs, for example, move the promise toward a new international outlook. A political vision of peacemaking, including issues of security and justice, is made available and accessible to the nations. The focus of the promise is most clearly stated in Isaiah 49:6, where the Lord gives his servant as a light to the nations.

—from Ivan D. Friesen, *Isaiah*, Believers Church Bible Commentary (Scottdale, Pa: Herald Press, 2009), 17–19. Used by permission.

Session format

In this volume on Isaiah, you will find eight sessions for either group or individual use. The easy-to-use format starts with an in-depth Bible study and ends with seven short devotionals designed to be read in the days after the session. Here's a guide to each session:

- **Opening:** The opening of the Bible study portion calls you into the session through a summary of the text and a few questions for reflection. Before you begin each session, take time to read the text reflectively.

- **For the leader:** These are ideas for how to use the material in a group setting. If using the material individually, omit this section.

- **Understanding God's Word:** This section makes connections made between the session's text and today's world.

- **Connecting with God's Word:** This is the heart of the guide; it's the in-depth Bible study that calls you to examine specific parts of the session's text. The writer gives background for a few verses of text, then outlines a series of questions for personal reflection or discussion. These questions always invite you to make connections between the biblical text and your own life.

- **Closing:** The Bible study portion of the session then closes with a brief time of worship and wrapping up.

- **Devotionals:** Immediately after the sessions you will find seven short devotionals on the session's text. Each devotional starts with a Scripture verse, includes a meditation, and ends with a prayer. Use these seven inspiring devotionals in the days after the session as way to keep the text in your heart and mind.

Spend time *With the Word* today!

Commitment to change

Isaiah 6:1-13

Opening

We worship a holy God. Reflect on how God's holiness impacts your faith. Sing or read a hymn, such as "Holy, Holy, Holy, Lord God Almighty," number 120 in *Hymnal: A Worship Book* (Scottdale, Pa: Mennonite Publishing House, 1992) or "Santo, Santo, Santo," number 400 in *Hymnal: A Worship Book.*

Understanding God's Word

A prophetic call story seems important for each of the major prophets, as it is for numerous leaders of Israel, including Abraham (Genesis 12), Moses (Exodus 3 and 6), and Samuel (1 Samuel 3). Jeremiah 1 recounts his sense of being called even before his birth. Ezekiel 1 is an elaborate attempt to describe the appearance of an indescribable revelation of the Lord. Isaiah's call narrative in Isaiah 6 corresponds to Jeremiah's and Ezekiel's and those of other great people of God.

The prophet Isaiah was active from 742 to about 701 BC. Thus Isaiah served before and after the fall of the Northern Kingdom to the Assyrians in 722 BC. And he is still around when the Assyrians almost take Jerusalem in 701 BC after capturing all of the other walled cities of Judah. This historical-political background helps stress that the task of the messenger is a difficult

For the leader

1. Bring artistic images which represent God or holiness and place them around the room, or light a candle or lamp in the room.

2. Ask someone to read Isaiah 6. Invite everyone else to listen for what stands out to them. What words or images grab their attention? Share briefly around the circle.

one with an unpleasant word to deliver. Experiencing the awesome presence of Yahweh is so overwhelming that Isaiah is moved to volunteer for service, barely realizing the difficulties.

Connecting with God's Word
"Seeing" God
Isaiah sees the Lord, Adonai, and goes on to describe what he sees. How do you describe an experience for which ordinary words and normal human categories are inadequate? Any attempt to sketch or paint such an appearance of God, including the ones in Ezekiel 1 and 10 and Revelation 4, will come up short. What are we to make of these living creatures with wings, faces, and eyes?

There are elements in Isaiah 6—fire, smoke, shaking, a voice, perhaps thunder, and bright light—that connect with Mt. Sinai (Exodus 19), the dedications of the Tabernacle (Exodus 40) and Temple (2 Chronicles 7), or even Pentecost (Acts 2) and Paul's conversion (Acts 9). We search for language and images from our ordinary experiences, but here they fail us. The essential matter is that Isaiah encountered God, that Isaiah received a glimpse of God's glory.

The seraphs, *seraphim* in Hebrew, are presented as ministering beings around or above the Lord. The Hebrew scriptures occasionally mention Yahweh's council or court as in Psalm 82:1, 89:7, 1 Kings 22:19-22, and Jeremiah 23:18. Did God's people borrow this picture from the Canaanite pantheon and its assembly of the gods known from Ugarit in 14th-century BC northern Syria in order to describe their heavenly reality? There, El sits as father of the gods. The Hebrew *Yahweh Sabaoth*, is often translated as "the Lord of hosts." The hosts are often explained as God's armies or angels, and are perhaps a dim reflection of the lesser gods surrounding El of the Canaanites.

Using the words "holy, holy, holy" three times is a way to call God superlatively most holy. At this pronouncement, the building shook and the place filled with smoke—more power and mystery.

- Recall times when you had a dream that was almost impossible to put into words. Have you experienced God's awesome holiness, or power, in ways difficult to describe?

- This image of God on a throne surrounded by courtiers seems to compare God to the powerful rulers of that time. How is God like these rulers and how is God different? What kind of power does God have and how does God use it?

- What images of God are common in our culture? What do they convey about God's power? How do they challenge the "ruling powers" of our time?

Feeling unclean

An overwhelmed Isaiah confesses his own unworthiness and uncleanness in the presence of this holy God. Isaiah feels inadequate before the Lord of hosts, "LORD Almighty" (NIV). In Isaiah's state of unworthiness a seraph purifies him with a burning coal, removes his guilt, and atones for his sin. With special attention to mouth and lips, the seraph is already preparing Isaiah for his mission of communication, even before he volunteers.

- When do you experience a sense of unworthiness?
- Why is speech (clean lips) so important? Where do you long for truth to be spoken and heard in our homes, communities, and nations?
- Read Matthew 13:13-17. How does Jesus' life and teaching help us to see and hear who God is and what God is saying to us?

Commitment to God

Yahweh said, "Who will go?" Isaiah said, "Send me" (6:8). The question becomes, "Who will go for us?" The "us" may refer to the seraphs-hosts-angels-lesser gods surrounding Yahweh. The "us" may also connect to the "plural of majesty." In 6:1, "Lord" in lower case letters is Adonai, which can mean literally "my lords."

In such a grand setting, how can Isaiah not willingly fit into God's program? "Here am I" is a typical obedient response when God calls (Abraham, Genesis 22:1-11; Moses, Exodus 3:4; Samuel, 1 Samuel 3:4; Mary, Luke 1:38; and Ananias, Acts 9:10). "I hear you; you have my attention, and I am at your service," is followed by the willing words, "Send me."

- In what sense has God called you? How are you responding to God's call on your life?
- What are the differences and similarities between a call to conversion and a call to special ministry and vocation? Can there be a special call for a specific task?

Closing

Reflect on where God is present in your life. How might God be calling you? Pray for ears to hear and eyes to see.

Devotionals

Devotional 1

In the year that King Uzziah died, I saw the LORD sitting on a throne, high and lofty; and the hem of his robe filled the temple.
—Isaiah 6:1

Can it really be? Isaiah is in the presence of the Creator of the universe, the One who strung all those stars in the sky—yet all he brings back is a fashion report?

Some might excuse Isaiah by saying that no words could convey the majesty of God. Also, these were turbulent times. A king had just died—one who had provided stability and remained faithful for a long time. Isaiah must have been unsettled and preoccupied.

Rather than criticize Isaiah, perhaps we should ask how we describe the people around us. Each one is made in the image of God. Each one gives us insight into God's way of thinking, acting, and loving. Yet so often we condense our impressions of each precious human being into a report of clothing, hairstyle, shoes. Every human we encounter provides a chance to encounter the mystery of the eternal. How about taking a real good look? —*Frank Ramirez*

Open my eyes, God of vision, that I might see with your eyes.

Devotional 2

I said: "Woe is me! I am lost, for I am a man of unclean lips . . . yet my eyes have seen the King, the LORD of hosts." —Isaiah 6:5

I expect visions of God to be beautiful, awesome, and uplifting. Isaiah's vision sounds like it was all of that, but it also overwhelmed him; he felt utterly unworthy.

I once went to hear a performance of Mozart's Requiem at the grandest cathedral in Seattle, prepared to be awed and moved. Yet we found ourselves sitting next to a sleeping, homeless man. I tried to be accepting, but instead became irritated as he continued sleeping.

When the music stopped, however, and the congregational responses began, the man sprang to his feet and recited the Latin liturgy from memory. When it came time to pass the peace, he shook our hands and welcomed us; we were visiting his church! I felt ashamed for misjudging this man, thinking he did not belong.

I expected to receive a lofty vision of God, but I also experienced Isaiah's feeling, "Woe is me." *–Janet Toews Berg*

God, you called Isaiah after he expressed his shame. Please accept my shortcomings and show me something of yourself today.

Devotional 3

I said: "Woe is me! I am lost, for I am a man of unclean lips, and I live among a people of unclean lips: yet my eyes have seen the King, the LORD of hosts." —Isaiah 6:5

I was only 20 when a minister came to lead deeper-life services. People from all over town flocked to the church. The atmosphere was charged with an almost tangible sense of the Almighty's presence.

What most caught my attention, however, was the action of the people. They got right with God as they responded with deep repentance. Even my parents, who had worked in church planting for several decades, found a new level of relationship with their Lord.

This is the closest parallel to Isaiah's experience I have encountered. People felt like they had "unclean lips" because they were meeting the King. Yet, it was a time of renewal as they had an honest encounter with God.

A friend once suggested that true worship occurs when we tell the truth to God about ourselves. Telling the truth can have a wonderful releasing effect that can result in a deeper, closer walk with God.
–David Wiebe

O God, I come to you as I am and commit myself to you. Cleanse me and make me fit for your service. Renew my spirit daily, and thank you for your love.

Devotional 4

The seraph touched my mouth . . . and said: "Now that this has touched your lips, your guilt has departed and your sin is blotted out." —Isaiah 6:7

During a church retreat, participants were asked to stop at several stations to remember the ways we had sinned against God and others. At each station we picked up a weight to place in a bag.

I like to think of myself as a good person, but the weight of my bag made me want to cry out like Isaiah, "Woe me! I am lost . . ."

When we were finally able to drop our "sins" at the foot of the cross, what a sense of release swept over me! I wanted to tell everyone of the forgiveness and mercy I had received!

Isaiah encountered God's glory and immediately remembered his unworthiness. Yet the holiness of God is not sullied by Isaiah's presence. Rather, it transforms Isaiah. He is set free from sin and guilt. This cleansing is also a commission; Isaiah is sent out to spread God's word among the people. –*Matt Hamsher*

Thank you, God, for setting me free from my sin and guilt. Help me share your love and truth with others.

Devotional 5

Then I heard the voice of the Lord saying, "Whom shall I send, and who will go for us?" And I said, "Here am I; send me!" —Isaiah 6:8

At times I feel overwhelmed when I see the needs of people all around me. How can God use me to make a difference?

Before Isaiah can do God's work, God has to equip him. Isaiah needs a fresh vision of God. Salvation is God's work. No need is too big for God. No person is too lost for God's love.

When Isaiah sees God's holiness he feels lost. Our response might be similar: "I haven't got what it takes. I am no better than the people who need my help."

Isaiah's confession leads to repentance and cleansing. Not by ceremonial washing, lengthy prayers, or painful penance. Isaiah's cleansing is God's work. God has the remedy for the sin and brokenness in us and others.

God calls us to be cleansed ourselves, then to tap into Christ, the source of our strength, and to tell and show forth God's salvation. –*Helen Grace Lescheid*

God, cleanse me, fill me, and use me to show and tell people of your love today.

Devotional 6

Then I heard the voice of the Lord saying, "Whom shall I send, and who will go for us?" And I said, "Here am I; send me!"
—Isaiah 6:8

What does it mean to be called by God? For years, I have been writing about my call to be a pastor. I am trying to understand where and when, like Isaiah, I heard God. What led me to quit my job as a public school teacher and move my young family across the country to attend seminary with no concrete plans?

Isaiah's call is different from my own call, but I recognize common themes. When I left teaching, I felt lost, as did Isaiah in his first encounter with God. But along the way, I did hear a call and like Isaiah, responded, "Yes!"

As you read about Isaiah's call, reflect on yours. Ask what God is inviting you to do and to learn in this phase of your life.
–Larry Hauder

God of Isaiah, thank you for inviting me on a journey with you. Continue to show me your way and your will.

Devotional 7

"Here am I; send me!" —Isaiah 6:8

In these verses Isaiah plumbs the depths and the heights of spiritual experience. Nothing is more harrowing than standing before God in all our pettiness, selfishness, greed, and hatred. Isaiah wails, "Woe is me! . . . For I am a man of unclean lips." This experience doesn't destroy Isaiah, however. God cleanses him so that he is ready to say, "Here am I; send me."

This experience shaped Isaiah's work as a prophet. His job included speaking words of judgment to the people. He would understand how people felt; he'd known sin firsthand, too. Similarly, because he had experienced the cleansing power of God, he could speak words of hope with conviction.

Unfortunately, it doesn't always work this way in my life. Sometimes I catch myself harshly judging people. Isaiah's words remind us that forgiveness is a miraculous gift of God. Receiving grace is a mountaintop experience. Are we ready to be sent out to share that message?
–Carol Penner

Thank you, Lord, for helping me to confront my need for your grace. Thank you for equipping me to share your good news of grace in Christ Jesus.

God's people comforted

ISAIAH 40

Opening

This chapter marks a dramatic shift in the prophet Isaiah's message. After experiencing years of desolation and exile, the people now hear an amazing word of hope and deliverance. Read Lamentations 1:1-3, 16-18, and notice how often the theme "no one to comfort" shows up. Then listen to a recording of "Comfort, Comfort Ye" from Handel's *Messiah*, or sing "Comfort, Comfort O My People," number 176 in *Hymnal: A Worship Book* (Scottdale, Pa: Mennonite Publishing House, 1992). What feelings do these words stir up? What questions do you have?

Understanding God's Word

As noted in the opening, there is a significant change in tone and message in this chapter. Scholars believe that the first 39 chapters of Isaiah came from a difficult time in Judah's history when they lived under the constant threat of Assyria and Egypt's military forces. Indeed, in 701 BC, the Assyrian king Sennacherib invaded Judah to quell a revolt and took

For the leader

1. Review the historical background briefly, and what the Jewish people experienced after the Babylonians destroyed Jerusalem and took many of the people captive.
2. Invite everyone to remember a time when they felt desolate and far from home. What was helpful to them at that time?
3. Isaiah 40 is a long chapter, so start by focusing on the first 11 verses. Four voices are heard, so ask four people to read the different parts: verses 1-2, 3-5, 6a and 9-11, and 6b-8. Ask everyone to specifically notice the words and images of comfort and reassurance.

control of many cities. Jerusalem, however, was spared until 586, when Nebuchadnezzar destroyed the temple and took many of the people into captivity in Babylon.

By contrast Isaiah 40–66, the last chapters of the book, appear to be written during and after this time of exile. Jerusalem was ruined and those exiled longed for their country. They struggled to understand why this had happened to them and how to remain faithful to God when they could no longer worship in the temple. They also had to deal with the reality of Babylonian gods and Babylonian ways, which appeared so much more dominant than their own.

Yet, God was bringing a message of hope. Babylon's power had weakened after the death of Nebuchadnezzar, and Cyrus the Persian seemed to represent the possibility of change. Perhaps God would use Cyrus to end their time of exile and let them return home.

Connecting with God's Word

A second prophetic call

Just as Isaiah 6 pictures God presiding over a heavenly council, here again God appears enthroned above the earth (vv. 12-17, 22-23, and 26-28) and attended by heavenly beings. They call out to one another, declaring God's glory, and urge the prophet to go to the people with the good news of God's comfort and plan to deliver them.

Once again, the prophet is reluctant: "What shall I cry? All people are grass, their constancy is like the flower of the field . . ." Perhaps their lips have been cleaned up, yet they are still transitory and unreliable.

Nevertheless, the heavenly court is insistently hopeful. No longer is the message one of impending doom. This time the call announces hope and reassures the people that God is still the great Creator and able to bring about deliverance, despite any evidence to the contrary. The announcement of "good tidings" in verse 9 could also be translated "gospel" or "good news" as in Mark 1:1. The normal setting is that of a king announcing good news of victory over one's enemies. So the prophet is announcing God's impending "victory" over their captors, and subsequent blessing for the people.

- Which is easier to give, a message of doom or one of hope? Which is easier to believe?

- Think of a time you received a message of hope that seemed too good to be true. What evidence did you look for? What is necessary for hope to have a solid foundation?

God, the great Creator

Read the rest of the chapter, noting a primary emphasis on God as Creator. There are numerous links back to Genesis 1, such as the breath of God blowing over the earth (vv. 7 and 24), God's word speaking with power (vv. 8 and 26), and God measuring out the waters, the heavens, and the dust of the earth (v. 12).

The overall message is that just as God created the world in the beginning, God is doing another, amazing new thing. God is recreating life again, this time in the midst of history and great loss. Even more, God's power to create is much stronger than that of any empire. Even the violent, powerful social and political system of Babylon will not last. Next to God, the nations are mere ". . . dust on the scales" (v. 15).

- Who announces such a message today? Is it received as a promise or perceived more as a threat?
- How does your congregation demonstrate faith in God's creative power over the nations?

The good shepherd

A comforting image in this chapter is that of God as a loving, gentle shepherd (v. 11). In Ezekiel 34:1-16 and John 10:11-16, Israel's leaders are pictured as careless and ruthless shepherds who exploit the sheep or leave them helpless before the wolves.

By contrast, God promises to strengthen and empower those who are weak and vulnerable. God feeds, carries, and accompanies. Indeed, in this image, God is more like a nurturing mother than a mighty creator or warrior. But these qualities are also powerful. They, too, are needed to create and sustain life.

- What is your image of a leader? What qualities do you look for? How does this compare to the tasks listed in these passages?
- How does your congregation encourage and honor the nurturing qualities given in this picture of a shepherd?

Closing

Listen to "He Shall Feed His Flock Like a Shepherd" from Handel's *Messiah*. Pray for one another, that in times of despair and pain, we might find hope in God's power to bring new life and deliverance.

Devotionals

Devotional 1

Comfort, O comfort my people, says your God. —Isaiah 40:1

I love this picture, of God calling for messengers to comfort the people and speak tenderly to them. It's a bit like when Jesus declared that he longed to gather the people "together as a hen gathers her brood under her wings" (Matthew 23:37). Clearly, God wants to bring reassurance and protection to those who are mourning, who are dealing with great loss, or who are struggling to survive.

It's hard to remember this, though, when facing difficulty myself. God can feel so far away. Perhaps that's why God asked for messengers, human companions who could go to the people, and share this good news directly. Truly, comfort comes best from those who have faced similar situations and are willing to share the pain. This is why Jesus' life among us is so powerful. He walked and suffered with us, in order to share God's message of deep, tender love.
–Linda Gehman Peachey

Loving God, thank you for walking with us in Jesus; and thank you for friends who continue to share your comfort and love.

Devotional 2

Every valley shall be lifted up, and every mountain and hill be made low. —Isaiah 40:4a

These words are so familiar that it's easy to forget how difficult this would be. To have whole mountains disappear? Or made level with the valleys? How could this be done without massive disruption?

But I guess that's the point. Those who are suffering want major change. And this is not about the landscape; it's about social change and political upheaval.

Hannah declares, "The Lord makes poor and makes rich; he brings low, he also exalts" (1 Samuel 2:7). Mary, too, affirms that God "has brought down the powerful from their thrones, and lifted up the lowly" (Luke 1:52).

I admit I find myself both drawn toward, and yet cringing at, these words. Yes, there is so much in our world that should change–and drastically. But what would that mean for me? Where would I find myself then? Am I willing to live on a level playing field?
–Linda Gehman Peachey

Oh God, help us see the world as you do; and give us courage to participate in your work of leveling off the mountains and raising up the valleys.

Devotional 3

He will feed his flock like a shepherd; he will gather the lambs in his arms . . . and gently lead the mother sheep. —Isaiah 40:11

One picture I remember from my childhood was of Jesus as the Good Shepherd. He was surrounded by sheep and carried one in his arms. It was a good representation of this verse, and evoked a deep sense of tranquility and safety.

More recently, though, I have begun to realize just how remarkable this image is because it casts God in a very nurturing, caretaking role. What would a modern day "shepherd" look like in our context? A primary school teacher? A nurse? A mother feeding her young child? A father rocking his child to sleep?

Do we dare to see God this way? I'm afraid it's much easier to picture God as a mighty ruler, with a scepter in hand. Yet, these nurturing images are important. They help us see a side of God, and a side of leadership, that is too often missing in our world. *–Linda Gehman Peachey*

Dear God, thank you that you gather up the lambs and care for the mother sheep. Help us to follow your example.

Devotional 4

Even the nations are like a drop from a bucket, and are accounted as dust on the scales. —Isaiah 40:15

My country is in the midst of a presidential election campaign. Of course, many things are said during such campaigns, but one statement especially caught my ear. One of the candidates asserted that the "destiny of our nation is greatness, exceptionalism." Obviously, he does not think of the United States as a "drop" of water or piece of "dust!" And I'm sure he is not alone.

Yet, God knows that our nation is but one among many. It will not last forever. Even our vast military might cannot guarantee our safety or give us happiness. Like many nations and empires before us, our power will wane and be replaced by others.

It's essential, then, to place our faith in God and to follow God's way, even when this differs from the ways of the nations. For God's love will last forever, long after we become dust. *–Linda Gehman Peachey*

Dear God, help us remember that we are human; we are not God. Help us trust and follow your way.

Devotional 5

Lift up your eyes on high and see: Who created these? He who brings out their host and numbers them, calling them all by name; because he is great in strength, mighty in power, not one is missing. —Isaiah 40:26

Here again the prophet paints a comforting image of God. But this time God is a mighty Creator, who puts the stars and planets in the sky and keeps them all in place. It's as if God is a cosmic shepherd, tending to all the hosts of heaven and making sure none are lost.

Not only that, but God numbers them and calls each one by name. God is the amazing Creator, "great in strength, mighty in power," yet also able to pay attention to and care for each created being.

As humans, it is hard to hold all this together. Indeed, to whom can we compare this God (v. 25)? It is certainly reassuring that the God we worship uses God's great strength and power to make sure that "not one is missing." –Linda Gehman Peachey

Dear God, thank you for your amazing power and creativity, and how you use this in caring, attentive ways throughout the vast expanses of the universe.

Devotional 6

He gives power to the faint, and strengthens the powerless. —Isaiah 40:29

One of the most inspiring stories I've encountered recently is that of Leymah Gbowee and her work with the women of Liberia to bring an end to the violence there. If any group demonstrates the truth of this verse, it is these women.

They had no power whatsoever, as normally understood. Nevertheless, they used the power they had to stand together day after day, and in all kinds of weather, demanding that their leaders listen to their concerns and respond. When peace negotiations were finally started, they traveled to the site of the peace talks, spoke out courageously, and held their leaders accountable. They used their strength, their faith, and their solidarity to bring a measure of peace to their communities.

Truly God's understanding is unsearchable (v. 28): giving strength and inspiration in amazing ways to those often considered faint and powerless.
–Linda Gehman Peachey

Dear God, help us trust in you and in the strength you give. Keep us from despair but help us find and use your wisdom and courage.

Devotional 7

Those who wait for the LORD shall renew their strength . . . they shall run and not be weary, they shall walk and not faint. —Isaiah 40:31

I confess I have often sung these words without thinking much about what they mean. It is also tempting to focus on the latter part of the verse, about running without weariness. Yet the emphasis is really on the first phrase: waiting for the Lord.

It is essential to listen to God, and do the hard work of discernment to see where God is at work and how we might join in. This takes much patience and persistence, and a willingness to trust in the small steps. We are not God and don't have to accomplish the whole journey, but simply follow the portion of the path we've been given, trusting God and those who follow us to continue the work and bring it to completion. We can take one step at a time, relying on God for strength, wisdom, and energy.
–Linda Gehman Peachey

Strong and faithful God, help us to wait on you, listening for your guidance and trusting you to lead us day by day.

Recreating community

Isaiah 43:1-13

Opening

Reflect on a time when you felt as if you, or those close to you, were walking through fire or deep water. How did you experience comfort and reassurance? How have you shared this experience with others?

Understanding God's Word

Just prior to this chapter, the nation of Israel is described as a blind and deaf people who would not follow in the ways of the Lord. The Lord punished them by allowing Israel to be plundered and looted by her enemies. But Israel still "did not understand"; nor did she "take it to heart" (42:25). But now, the Lord is preparing to do a new thing (42:9-10, 14-16).

God promises to be with them, redeem them, and bring them back from exile. God will also call on them to witness to all the nations of God's saving power. They are to help those are who are blind to see, and those who are deaf to hear and understand (43:8-10).

For the leader

1. Give everyone paper and pencil. Ask them to draw a picture of what it would mean to walk through deep waters or through fire. Invite those who are willing to share either their picture or something about their experience.

2. Ask one person to read Isaiah 43:1-7, and another to read 8-13. Notice the change in tone and content.

Connecting with God's Word

"I will be with you" (43:1-2)

"Waters" and "fire" are both literal and symbolic references. The actual waters of the Red Sea posed a fearful threat during the escape from Egypt. And God's wrath is often seen as fire, or can refer to how warring nations destroy a people and its possessions (Psalm 66:12, 74:7).

The proof of the promise always lies in the record of the past. Look into history and understand! Who created you as a people? Who formed you into a functioning society? Who redeemed you from trouble? Who summoned you by name and became your guardian and protector?

Since the answer to these questions is "the Lord God," the people should have nothing to fear. Past history gives authoritative reason for a future better than what Israel had suffered so far. God had not forsaken the people of Israel nor cast them aside.

- What guarantees come to us when we belong to the people of God? Is it true that God, the Creator, Sustainer, and Redeemer of Israel, will protect people come what may, whether flood or fire? It is sure that everyone will face physical death. So what is God's guarantee concerning protection from disaster?

- Isaiah 43:2 suggests three abiding truths: (1) God will never forsake us, but will go with us when we pass through troubled waters; (2) God will encourage us to keep a strong trust in God when the floods of life want to overwhelm us; and (3) although fire may destroy the flesh, it cannot consume the soul, which is nurtured and kept eternally by the Lord God. Which of these three truths of God's guarantee do you find most meaningful?

To these three truths we should add a fourth, which applies to the community as a whole. The guarantee to Israel and to God's people today, is that the community of faith will not be wiped out. The people of Jacob will live on from generation to generation. The church of Jesus Christ will prevail, even against the gates of hell (Matthew 16:18).

- To what extent can the people of Israel—or Christians—today claim God's promises of protection and preservation as a *community* of faith?

"You are my witnesses" (43:10)

The community of Israel had been chosen by the Lord to be a servant (see also 41:9; 42:1) and witness to the Lord (43:10, 12; and 44:8). The role of a witness was to testify by making statements of truth based on what the people had experienced, observed, and seen.

The credentials for their role as witnesses came in several ways. They had experienced redemption from Egypt, so they had a story of salvation to tell. They had received a special calling through the covenant that God made with them at Mount Sinai, so they could testify to a special relationship with God. God had protected them in their wilderness wanderings, which gave them good reason for pointing to the graciousness of their Lord. On the basis of this experiential evidence, the people could bear witness that there is only one Savior (43:11); only one God (43:12).

- Review this passage again and identify the message assigned to God's witnesses.
- Write or speak a statement of public witness for our day that would be faithful to the content of the message by Isaiah found in this text.

Closing

Read Isaiah 43:1-3 together as a promise to take with you through the coming days. Sing together "When Peace, Like a River," number 336 in *Hymnal: A Worship Book* (Scottdale, Pa: Mennonite Publishing House, 1992).

Devotionals

Devotional 1

Do not fear, for I have redeemed you; I have called you by name, you are mine.
—Isaiah 43:1

Youngsters were interviewed about how they could tell if someone really loved them. "That's easy," replied one child. "When somebody loves you, the way they say your name is different. You know your name is safe in their mouth."

God "calls" each of us by name to build a relationship. God wills to redeem us, offers nearness in difficult circumstances (v. 2), makes effort to enrich our present life (v. 4), and assures a secure future (v. 5).

My older brother is recovering from open-heart surgery. These days my emails are full of family members' prayers and well-wishes forwarded throughout our vast family system. No message goes unread.

The ultimately important thing is that God speaks my name and your name and our loved ones' names with absolute concern and care. It's a comfort to know God knows our name. We couldn't be any safer.
–Doug Schulz

Lord, as I call out to you today for my needs and those of others, may I remember who you are. Then I will know who I am to you.

Devotional 2

When you pass through the waters, I will be with you; and the rivers, they shall not overwhelm you. —Isaiah 43:2

Passing through the Red Sea was a defining moment for the people of Israel. Now, in another time of national crisis, Isaiah reminds Israel that God will deliver them even as they were delivered from slavery in Egypt.

Yet water creates fear. There are invisible undercurrents and unknown creatures lurking beneath the surface. Even the most placid body of water has claimed its victims.

Several weeks after our son, Tim, drowned, our other son was baptized by immersion. I vividly remember watching him go under the water and for an instant, I relived Tim's death. As he emerged from this watery grave, I also experienced the hope of the resurrection.

Adversity and suffering are dangerous waters. They take us out of our comfort zone. We long to return to familiar territory. Yet, because God has created and redeemed us, we need not fear. God will be with us. –*Keith Harder*

Lord, grant me courage and faith to go through the waters that are before me, confident that you will be with me.

Devotional 3

I am the LORD your God, the Holy One of Israel, your Savior. —Isaiah 43:3

Israel turned away from God again and again. Now the Israelites find themselves captive to the Babylonians. Their temple is destroyed, the people scattered, and their leaders put to the sword.

What God chooses to remember about all this is remarkable! God remembers forming a people, in response to Israel's cry from Egyptian bondage. God recounts their passing through the waters of the Red Sea and the crossing of the Jordan River. Then God plunges into an expression of deep love: "you are precious in my sight" (v. 4).

Memory can lead us in many directions. Whether we reflect on our own histories or those of our churches, we often run into pain, joy, and sorrow. God uses memory as a pathway to the heart, not to discount memory but redeem it. We may focus on current failures, but God helps us remember the long, continuous story of God's love for us. *–Jon Yoder*

Lord, your Word reminds us of how memory, love, and forgiveness are linked. May we grow more into your likeness.

Devotional 4

Do not fear, for I have redeemed you; I have called you by name; you are mine. . . . You are precious in my sight, and honored. —Isaiah 43:1, 4

"Are hugs here?" my son often asked as a child. At times he asked me to sit down so he could snuggle in my lap. Other times he shared concerns, hurts, or fears.

For me, today's passage feels like a big hug from God. How reassuring to read that God knows my name, and I am precious and honored in God's sight! No matter what my difficulties, I need not fear, because God walks through them with me (vv. 2, 5). I can share concerns, joys, and problems and know I will be heard and cared for. Whether joyful or sad, God has time to sit with me. As I draw near and ask, "Are hugs here?" the answer is always, "Yes, Lydia, an abundant yes."

What are you facing today? No matter what you're experiencing, why not curl up with God's Word and receive a big divine hug? *–Lydia Siemens Harris*

Loving God, how wonderful to know I'm precious to you and that you always have time for me. Today I bring my concerns and rest in your loving arms.

Devotional 5

You are precious in my sight, and honored. — Isaiah 43:4

"Thank you! Thank you for telling me about Jesus!" the voice at the other end of the line said. "Jesus is always with me, so I am not alone."

Junko (not her real name) was calling from Japan. She would often refer back to when she walked by our church and read the sign, "Come to me, all you that are weary and are carrying heavy burdens, and I will give you rest" (Matthew 11:28).

Junko needed rest. Her husband had recently divorced her and she was heartbroken. She was also emotionally challenged, and her family put her into a mental institution for many years. Junko, however, clings to Jesus in faith, knowing that someday she will be whole again.

This passage reminds us we are all precious in God's sight. God doesn't look at our accomplishments, education, or status. God's love has redeemed and called each of us by name. *–Mary Derksen*

Thank you, God, for choosing me, and that I am precious in your sight.

* * * * * * * * * * * * * * *

Devotional 6

You are my witnesses, says the LORD, and my servant whom I have chosen.
—Isaiah 43:10

Cornelia Lehn once told of an unforgettable experience of speaking for God. As she started a bus trip, she prayed God would help her share her faith with others. A woman entered the bus who looked odd to Cornelia.

"Oh no, Lord!" she whispered. But the woman sat down beside her, lit her cigarette, and began asking spiritual questions. Because Cornelia's seatmate was hard of hearing, Cornelia had to shout her answers, and thus witnessed to everyone on the bus. At the end of the trip, the lady said, "God bless you, hon."

Witnessing to our faith is like a chain. The links may be a smile, a casserole, a song, a word of encouragement–the list goes on. Any one of these could complete a series of events that brings a person to faith in Christ. What words and actions of mine will be part of that chain today? *–Mary Derksen*

Thank you, God, for the gifts you give me to witness of your love. Help me to be faithful in walk and talk.

* * * * * * * * * * * * * * *

Devotional 7

You are my witnesses, says the LORD. I am God. —Isaiah 43:12-13

Imagine a courtroom drama. The director sets the stage, convenes the actors, and hands out the script. Our role is that of "witness." The gallery is jammed. An entire generation is trying to sort out, from all the claimants, who merits loyalty and trust. Who is to be believed? We are summoned to the box.

And what then? Are we mute when called to give our testimony? Perhaps we blather on about trivial things. Or maybe we tell what we have overheard, only to be told "Objection! Hearsay."

A former blind man in the Gospels offers a model for giving evidence: "One thing I do know . . . I was blind, now I see" (John 9:25).

What calamity has become an occasion of sweet healing? What folly has been redeemed? What failure or suffering has become a deep well of compassion? Let me give an account of that truth today.
–Jonathan Larson

Amazing grace, how sweet the sound, that saved a wretch like me! I once was lost, but now am found, was blind but now I see!
—John Newton

Restoration and blessing

Isaiah 43:14–44:8

Opening

This passage emphasizes God's offer of a new beginning. God is dispensing with the old and doing "a new thing." Have you ever wished for the chance to start over? Or perhaps you have had to begin again even when that was not your choice. What feelings did you have? What was good and what was difficult about the experience?

Understanding God's Word

This text continues the theme of comfort and hope which starts in chapter 40. God is not bound by the past, but is now creating new possibilities for the people of Israel. This is evident by the words "But now . . ." which open both chapters 43 and 44. God promises to release the people from exile, bless them, and allow them to return home. Despite their sin, despite their half-hearted worship, God is still with them, God still loves them, and God will forgive.

For the leader

1. Sing or read together, "This Is a Day of New Beginnings," number 640 in *Hymnal: A Worship Book* (Scottdale, Pa: Mennonite Publishing House, 1992).

2. This passage has a number of stanzas, but all in God's voice. Ask six volunteers to read these sections in turn: 43:14-15, 16-21, 22-24, 25-28; 44:1-5, 6-8. What words or themes recur? What is God saying to you or to your congregation?

Connecting with God's Word

"I am doing a new thing!"

Only God can reverse the direction of history. God had determined that the people should go into exile as a result of their unfaithfulness. But that was now in the past (43:18). The people had served their term in "prison." God was now "doing a new thing" (43:19)! Enough of wandering about aimlessly in the wilderness of confusion and despair! Enough of living in a barren and thirsty land! God was making "a way in the desert" and "streams in the wasteland." These are themes that indicate the return of exiles from the land of Babylon to their former Judean home. They are words spoken to a people who needed to recover their hope.

Like the time of exodus from slavery in Egypt, God will make a "way in the sea, a path in the mighty waters" (43:16) and lead them out of exile. Though it must have been hard to imagine how this could happen, there is reassurance in remembering the power God exercised in creating the world and the amazing miracles which led them out of slavery. There is also reassurance that God can and will forgive the sins which caused so much pain and suffering.

- If you were to ask God to do a "new thing," what would it be?
- How does your congregation proclaim and demonstrate this good news of restoration and new beginnings?

Bearing God's name

In Isaiah 43:1, God declares that "I have called you by name." However, in verse 22, God complains, "you did not call upon me." God showed them great love and great favor, but it was not returned. God had hoped for worship and acknowledgment, to be called by name, even though they were in exile. Yet, it appears too many of the people had adopted the ways of Babylon and worshiped its gods.

Still, God continues to seek those willing to take God's name (44:5). Walter Brueggemann notes that the Hebrew words in verse 5 have the sense of "belonging to." This was thought to be a stamp placed on a product when a tax was paid in kind, making clear that it now belonged to the king (Ivan D. Friesen, *Isaiah*, Believers Church Bible Commentary, Scottdale, Pa: Herald Press, 2009, 65). God reminds the people they do not belong to Babylon but to God. They have been stamped with God's name, and will return home where they belong.

- How do you show you have taken God's name and bear God's stamp? How does your congregation nurture an identity rooted in God, rather than in the surrounding culture?

Forget the past?

The Teacher who wrote Ecclesiastes said, "For everything there is a season, and a time for every matter under heaven . . . a time to seek and a time to lose" (3:1, 6a). In line with this advice, our text would support the idea that there's a time to remember and a time to forget; a time to dwell on the past and a time to look ahead to the new that's coming. Some of us have a tendency to get wrapped up in the past. Others of us are visionaries, dreaming of how the future could be. We need both kinds of input in the Christian community. It depends very much on what the deliberations of the moment require by way of upholding faith and faithfulness.

- Who are the historians, and who are the visionaries, in your congregation? How does each contribute to the faith and faithfulness of the congregation?
- How does your congregation nurture both types of input?

Closing

Recite 43:18-19 together as a promise to take with you into the week:

> "Do not remember the former things,
>   or consider the things of old.
> I am about to do a new thing;
>   now it springs forth,
>   do you not perceive it?
> I will make a way in the wilderness
>   and rivers in the desert."

Devotionals

Devotional 1

Thus says the LORD, who makes a way in the sea, a path in the mighty waters . . .
—Isaiah 43:16

During a visit to Haiti, I went sailing. This was forbidden, but I did it anyway. All went smoothly until we set out for deeper water. Then the wind and waves whipped our sailboat beyond control, and we capsized. At the last second, my friend wrested me from under the boat and dumped me on top of its upside-down belly.

The relief I felt symbolizes the hope in this passage. Because of their rebellion, God allowed the Israelites to be held captive in Babylon. Isaiah reminds them that the God who redeemed them once—from Pharaoh—will redeem them again; although this time they will be saved from their own sin, not the sin of others. It is easy to curse the waves, rather than admit that we chose the dangerous waters. I still feel shame that I went sailing.

Yet, God's mercy can transform all our choices into "new things." –*Laurie Oswald Robinson*

God of Israel and my Creator, transform my choices today. Let them witness to your grace and bring praise to your name.

Devotional 2

Do not remember the former things, or consider the things of old. —Isaiah 43:18

A friend generously offered me his cottage for a week of silent retreat before I entered seminary. The name of the cottage was "New Beginnings." How appropriate! I had opened my life to new beginnings.

In our text God recounts the protection given the Israelites. God, however, tells the people, "Do not remember the former things, or consider the things of old." God is about to do a new thing, to give the people a new beginning.

Brain scientists say that some 50,000 thoughts pass through our minds daily. When we linger too long on one or expand it to unreal proportions, we can become paralyzed. Only in letting go of these destructive thought patterns can there be room for new ideas and solutions. It is easy to replay old memory tapes. We can lock others and ourselves into thought and behavior patterns that stunt rather than stimulate growth. –*Elizabeth Raid*

God of new beginnings, redeem us from destructive ways so that we may receive the many blessings you have prepared for us.

Devotional 3

I am about to do a new thing; now it springs forth, do you not perceive it? —Isaiah 43:19a

While the author of Ecclesiastes writes that there is nothing new under the sun (Ecclesiastes 1:9), Isaiah tells us God is in the business of new possibilities. Both offer sage advice. On the one hand, we are urged to see the continuity of human experience and take a humble view of our own perspective. On the other, we are urged to look for the fresh ways God breaks into our experience and offers new possibilities.

Recently, we celebrated our daughter's wedding. Though an ancient institution, every marriage represents something new and unique. So we pray our daughter and her husband may benefit from what others have learned, and also perceive the new thing that has been created through their marriage.

The newness spoken of in Isaiah 43 is grounded in God's grace and forgiveness. New possibilities break in upon us when we embrace the assurance of God's everlasting love. *–Keith Harder*

Lord, help me to perceive the new possibilities and opportunities that will come my way this day.

Devotional 4

I will make a way in the wilderness and rivers in the desert. —Isaiah 43:19b

In 2003, the United States led an invasion of Iraq during the Lenten season. Years later, we see its legacy: huge losses of life and more terror in a nation already wracked with violence.

Isaiah 43 prods us to review violence and repent. In verses 16-17, God reminds Israel that it was not their military prowess, but God, who made a path through the sea so they could cross unharmed by Pharaoh's army. Today, too, God offers a "new thing" to replace our old, futile ways.

God wants to unravel the ancient law of "eye for an eye" and do a new thing (v. 19). Can we let God work through Jesus, the Prince of Peace, and not set our own madness in motion again? God invites us to drink of this river of peace in the midst of the deserts of conflicts in our homes, churches, and nations.
–Laurie Oswald Robinson

God of all nations, we repent of our thirst for violence. Make us channels of Christ's peace, providing streams in the desert.

Devotional 5

The wild animals honor me, the jackals and the owls, because I provide water in the desert . . . to give drink to my people, my chosen. —Isaiah 43:20 (NIV)

Jackals don't have the greatest reputation. These scavengers are seen as cowardly opportunists who dine on the kills of other predators. But jackals may not deserve this bad image as their diet includes fruits, reptiles, birds, and carrion. Their family life is stable and both parents have important roles.

It is, perhaps, easier to like owls. The expression "wise as an owl" is used frequently, reminding us that owls have an excellent reputation. Most are beautiful and also skilled hunters.

That Isaiah would mention owls and jackals in the same breath as wild animals who give honor to God, shows that all animals are loved by God, and they, in turn, give praise and honor to their Creator. It also reminds us that praise ought to be as natural for all humans, no matter their circumstances or reputation, as it is for the rest of God's creatures. *—Bob Hoffman*

This is my Father's world; the birds their carols raise; the morning light, the lily white; declare their Maker's praise.
—Maltbie D. Babcock

Devotional

I, I am He who blots out your transgressions for my own sake, and I will not remember your sins. —Isaiah 43:25

Every New Year, some of us make resolutions to break bad habits, or start new regimes of exercise and proper eating. A new year can be a time to make a fresh start.

Isaiah told the people of Israel that God would give them a clean slate. Where there was despair, there would be new possibilities—a way in the wilderness and rivers in the desert.

Isaiah 43:22-24 are realistic about the people's offenses. Yet God will blot out their sins and remember them no more.

God extends to us the same gracious promise of forgiveness and restoration. We may not be in exile, but sin always creates distance between us and God. As we confess our sins and turn from them, God deletes those stains from the pages of our lives, offering us the joy of God's "new thing," with possibilities for lush growth where there was barrenness. *—Nancy Witmer*

Lord, I confess to you my sins. Thank you for giving me a fresh start and a clear conscience.

Devotional

Do not fear, O Jacob my servant . . . I will pour my spirit upon your descendants, and my blessings on your offspring.
—Isaiah 44:2-3

I wonder what it is like to be an older member of a congregation. What does it mean to watch the younger generations rise up and take leadership? Are there fears that what has been so deliberately and prayerfully built and established might someday be destroyed?

God's Word reassures us that we need not be afraid. God is working to establish a new generation of leaders, a people who will be renewed, strengthened, and empowered by God. God's Spirit is as much present and eager to anoint this younger generation, and the generations to come, as it has the former generations.

How can those who are older support and encourage the younger generation so that their growth and that of the church can continue? Let us be assured that God is indeed preparing to pour God's Spirit on a dry and thirsty generation. In fact, God is already doing it. *—Jill Landis*

God, assure us that we need not fear when you are pouring your Spirit on the future generations and on the leaders of our church.

Strength from God

Isaiah 49:5-6; 50:4-9

Opening

Think of a time when you felt God had given you a task that was too large or too difficult. How did you respond? What gave you strength and courage to begin or continue the assignment?

Understanding God's Word

Isaiah 40–55 are some of the loftiest texts in Scripture. They exude hope and new life for the Lord's people, fueled by God, who imagines and acts "outside the box." But these chapters also include sobering realities, as the four Servant Songs make clear.

This passage includes two of the Servant Songs. The others are in Isaiah 42:1-4 and Isaiah 52:13–53:12. Isaiah 42 identified the servant's mission as bringing justice and light to the nations; and that the servant will be gentle and the task will require perseverance.

In the song in Isaiah 49, the servant expresses failure (49:4). We do not know whether this is real or only a perception. But failure is not hard to imagine in an exilic circumstance. Isaiah 42:14–43:7 shows that captivity

For the leader

1. Explain that these verses come from two of the four "Servant Songs" in Isaiah. Ask one person to read the passage, while everyone else listens carefully. What is the overall message? What is surprising, disturbing, or comforting in these verses?

2. Invite those who are willing to share reflections from times they felt especially challenged by a task or situation. What was helpful to them?

had exacted a high toll from the refugees. Isaiah 44:9-20 points to the taint of idolatry that may have tempted the community of faith. A mission to such people could not have been easy.

The servant, however, doesn't linger over failure but immediately confesses renewed trust in God and receives renewed commissioning from the Lord. But the servant's recommissioning is not a reissuing of the original job description to restore the tribes of Israel to the Lord (49:5). This task is deemed "too light"—either too easy or too insignificant. God is "Creator of the ends of the earth" (40:28); how could the scope of God's salvation and the servant's task encompass anything less? Paul (and Barnabas) identified his mission to the Gentiles as a fulfillment of Isaiah's prophecy (see Acts 26:22-23).

Unfortunately, the servant again experiences resistance. Nevertheless, the servant does not receive adversity as a disconfirmation of his mission. Rather, adversity is an opportunity for determined faithfulness.

Connecting with God's Word

Light to the nations?
For the Judean exiles in Babylon, physical displacement and loss of identity shrink-wrapped their imagination and theology. The first round of God's "pastoral ministry" to the deportees involved comfort and tenderness (Isaiah 40:1-2). God's next step, however, was to blow the lid off their puny perspective ("too light!")!

Does God's "blowing off the lid" seem cruel? Well, the exiles had sunk from grief to capitulation. Eventually the bandaged skateboarder has to get back on the skateboard; the accident victim must get back behind the wheel. Continued coddling becomes disempowering. But "light to the nations"? That's a mighty high price; the freeway at rush hour. Ready or not, in Isaiah 49, God the therapist is out and God the dispatcher is in!

It sounds overwhelming. Yet God's method is well considered. Only those who have experienced vulnerability can help the vulnerable. It is the servant's obedient and determined witness—no matter what!—that is a light to the nations. This is not a judgmental, condescending, or sales-like posture but rather an enduring witness. God's light is not shone from afar *on* the world but embodied *in* the world. Vulnerable is valuable! Rather than *have* answers, God's servants *become* answers.

Reading Isaiah 49 and 50 together reminds us that in this present age God's light does not eliminate the darkness. Rather, God's light shines *through* the darkness. And the task of the servant is to remain faithful despite the difficulties.

5 • *Strength from God*

- How do you respond to the statement: "Only those who have experienced vulnerability can help the vulnerable?" How have you found this to be true, or not, in your life?

- Has there ever been a time when your discouragement was the result of thinking too small? How did you overcome it?

- Where does missional "small-mindedness" come from? Fear of failure? Fear that God will judge us for mistakes? Fear of squandering the church's resources? Fear of peer disapproval? How can we counter this?

Strength for the weary

Today, there are many kinds of weariness. There is weariness that comes from unmet hopes, longing for relief from depression, overcomplicated schedules, and conflicted relationships. The constant violent and tragic news on the media brings its own kind of weariness. And even the very best—living the alternative values of the kingdom of God—is wearying because it takes energy to be different.

Isaiah 40:27-31 announces God's strength for the weary and in Matthew 11:28-30, Jesus invites the weary to come to him and rest. In Isaiah 50:4, the servant ministers strength to the weary in words. Then in verses 7-9, the servant receives God's strength and issues a challenge to opponents. It is not a curse or judgment on them but a recognition of their vulnerability: Those who make *weary* will themselves *wear out*.

- What gives you hope in difficult times? What words sustain you when you are weary?

- Why might some oppose the servant's message, perhaps even those from the servant's own community?

- How have you responded to opposition or punishment because of your faith in God? What was especially helpful to you during those times?

Closing

Pray together for wisdom to see the immensity of God's vision for the world, and for courage to persevere during times of difficulty and despair. Sing together "The Work Is Thine, O Christ," number 396 in *Hymnal: A Worship Book* (Scottdale, Pa: Mennonite Publishing House, 1992).

Devotionals

Devotional 1

Now the Lord says, who formed me in the womb to be his servant . . . —Isaiah 49:5

I have always been fascinated with my birth story. My mother had a high-risk pregnancy causing her to be on bed rest for weeks in a hospital. This story reminds me that I am here for a purpose, and gives me trust that God will keep leading me.

Isaiah recounts a birth story of a servant of God and describes the servant's purpose: to bring, to gather, to raise up, and to restore the people of God. The call applies not only to the tribes of Jacob but to all nations, "that [God's] salvation may reach to the end of the earth."

We are all here by the hard-won miracle of birth. Each of our stories is unique and a reminder of God's love and intention for us. We must trust God's purpose to use us to bring, to gather, to raise up, and to restore the people of God. *—Patty Friesen*

God, thank you for tending me and loving me from before my birth; and help me as I find and live out your loving purpose for my life.

Devotional 2

The Lord God has given me the tongue of a teacher, that I may know how to sustain the weary with a word. —Isaiah 50:4

I recently visited my mother in a retirement community. I lived with her for a week, sharing meals with the residents and mingling with them. It soon became apparent who were the habitual complainers. They griped about cold food, foul weather, or few visitors.

But just as obvious were those who had a habit of speaking affirming words. They asked questions like "How did you sleep last night?" and said "Thank you" when the staff served meals or delivered medications.

I learned a valuable lesson. Words we choose to speak come from years of discipline, not from circumstances. Every resident had something they could complain about. Joints ached, health deteriorated, and independence was curtailed. Yet some had developed positive habits. They used speech "to sustain the weary."

Is it ever too late to begin training the tongue? I don't think so. I can begin today, exercising my words of affirmation and kindness. *—Larry Hauder*

Creator God, you who made us in your likeness, be patient with me as I learn to speak words to help the weary.

Devotional 3

The Lord God has given me the tongue of a teacher, that I may know how to sustain the weary with a word. —Isaiah 50:4

The last time it was my friend Marla. Once it was my mother. On another occasion, I received a sustaining word from the dean of the school where I was a student. Each time it happened I was weary from anxiety, lack of sleep, troubling questions, or a mountain that looked too big to climb.

Marla said, "You can do it!" My mother spoke not a word, simply reached over and gently squeezed my hand. The dean affirmed the direction I was heading. Each of them spoke with the tongue of a teacher. When we receive such encouragement, we know in our bones the blessing that comes from our teachers, whether or not we are in formal classrooms.

This text reminds us of our role as teacher and encourager. May we also remember that God is our helper, when we face humiliation and resistance. God always stands ready to help. *–Melissa Miller*

God, give us the tongue of a teacher. Sustain us when we are weary as we lean on you, our helper.

Devotional 4

I gave my back to those who struck me, and my cheeks to those who pulled out the beard; I did not hide my face from insult and spitting. —Isaiah 50:6

One of my most memorable experiences was visiting a priest in a tiny home in Guatemala City. He had once lived in a small rural community attacked by guerillas during Guatemala's civil war. Many were killed and others fled to the hills, surviving on what could be found in the wild. Some took up arms. Others, like him, believed that further violence would not bring peace.

The priest told his story with deep emotion and even some fear, yet his hope in God and love for others, even his enemies, shone through clearly. Like the teacher (v. 4) and like Jesus, he did not return violence for violence, but trusted God to make things right.

We may never flee for our lives or be beaten for our faith, yet we face other injustices. How will we respond? Will we plot revenge? Or will we put ourselves into the hands of God? *–Angela Reed*

Lord, help me not to retaliate if I am treated poorly for your sake, but trust you to defend me.

Devotional 5

The Lord God helps me; therefore I have not been disgraced; therefore I have set my face like flint. —Isaiah 50:7

In my childhood comic books, the hero was always the one who stood up to evil, who used super powers to overcome danger and dastardly villains.

There is part of me that is not quite satisfied with the picture of God's servant in this passage. Yes, the servant bore beatings and insults with quiet dignity. Yes, the servant was obedient to God. But is there more for someone looking for a hero?

Looking more closely, however, it took enormous faith to remain God's servant. When everything seemed to argue against God's care, when everything seemed to say that God had abandoned him, the servant still remained convinced of God's help. It took a super faith to say, "He who vindicates me is near" (v. 8a).

In Jesus' time people were also looking for a hero, someone to save them. Like the servant, Jesus met insult and death with a super faith in God. And God vindicated him in the resurrection. *–April Yamasaki*

O God, deepen my understanding of Jesus, your suffering servant, who is far greater than any superhero. Teach me to follow the servant's way.

Devotional 6

Who will contend with me? Let us stand up together. Who are my adversaries? Let them confront me. —Isaiah 50:8

Most of us can think of times when we stood up for our beliefs. I recall the beginning of the Gulf War, when a group of us held a prayer vigil outside city hall. While we meant to be quiet and peaceful, our location was a very public statement.

Soon, people in cars and trucks pulled up, honking their horns and waving American flags. People in fatigues surrounded us, chanting, and calling us names. As we fled the scene, our leader warned: "Don't go alone."

As I remember that day, I understand why people were upset. Many of them, no doubt, had family members putting their lives at risk. At the same time, I will never forget our convictions in opposing the violence of the war.

In this passage, Isaiah confesses there is nothing to fear: "God helps me . . . and I know that I shall not be put to shame" (v. 7). *–Ann Minter Fetters*

God, help me to know that you will stand by me, even if I am taking a risk doing what I believe is right.

Devotional 7

It is the Lord GOD who helps me; who will declare me guilty? —Isaiah 50:9

When my husband was in medical residency, he spent several nights a week at the hospital—and I hated it! It wasn't just the loneliness but the fact that he wasn't there to protect me. It seemed like every noise was an intruder. I would lie awake listening for the slightest indication something was wrong. Not a restful way to spend the night!

Finally I decided this was ridiculous. Often in the past I had relied on God to get me through hard times, and God had always been faithful. Why not ask God to give me rest now?

I gave God my fears and soon felt relieved that just as Mark was on call at the hospital, God was on call at home. God was watching over me, providing peace when I felt vulnerable and frightened. I was able to bask in the peace that comes from being connected to God. *–Dawn Mast*

Lord, I need to renew the communion with you that sometimes gets lost in the busyness of my day. Thank you for your peace that constantly sustains me.

5 · Strength from God

Trust God

Isaiah 51:1-16

Opening

Reflect on a time when you felt alone and forsaken by God. What brought comfort and reassurance? What do you still long to hear or see?

Understanding God's Word

It is important to remember the context of Isaiah 51. These words were addressed to a people in exile, a people in despair and needing a word of hope. It can be tempting to read these promises as addressed to a particular ethnic or religious group, but this can be dangerous, and used to justify the very things which God opposes. Though God chose the children of Israel, God's teaching goes out to everyone and God's justice is "a light to the peoples" (v. 4). God promises to release them from oppression and suffering, but they must not forget that God also opposed their own violence and injustice (Isaiah 1:15-17; 5:7-8).

For the leader

1. Display pictures of deserts and lush gardens to demonstrate the contrast between experiences of emptiness and desolation, and those of abundant life and joy.

2. Most of this passage is spoken by God so have one person read that voice (vv. 1-8, 12-16). Verses 9-11 are spoken by the people, so ask everyone else to read those verses together.

Connecting with God's Word

Listen, listen, listen

This word is repeated three times in Isaiah 51:1-8. It is similar to "hear" in Deuteronomy 6:4-5, the "Shema," a core Hebrew prayer, emphasizing that God alone is God. And this is the One we are to love with all our heart, soul, and might. Here God appeals to the people to listen, look, and remember; to have ears that truly hear and eyes to see God's work in the world, even in the midst of barrenness and desolation.

Interestingly, God's appeal to listen and look goes to those who pursue and know righteousness, those who have God's teaching in their hearts (vv. 1 and 7). It is not addressed to those who have never known God. Rather, those who think they understand God's ways may need to think again and reconsider how God works in the world.

So God reminds the exiled people of Abraham and Sarah. Certainly, these are great heroes of the faith. Yet, God emphasizes that Abraham was just one person when God called him. We also know that he was an immigrant, an "alien" who wandered into Egypt (Deuteronomy 26:5), and both were past child-bearing years when Sarah bore a son. So God works with situations that appear most improbable. God creates nations from what appear to be the most unlikely sources.

Finally, this teaching is paired with God's justice (v. 4). Indeed, righteousness and justice are linked together over 100 times in the Hebrew Scriptures, indicating that these qualities are intimately tied together. They demonstrate God's concern for right relationships with everyone, both God and our neighbors. Worship and ethics cannot be separated.

- How do you hear and remember God's actions in your life? Who helps you hear and see where God is at work?
- How do God's acts in the past give you courage and reassurance in the present? Where do you find hope in "hopeless" situations?
- How do you understand righteousness and justice? How are they similar and different? How are righteousness and justice lived out by your congregation?

Appeal to God and God's second response

This passage has two parts: an urgent plea to God for help in verses 9-11, and God's response in verses 12-16. The people even remind God of powerful acts done long ago. The references to Rahab and the dragon refer to chaos or mythological sea monsters which God subdued in creating beauty, life, and order on the earth (Genesis 1:1; Job 9:13, 26:12-13; Psalm 74:13-14, 89:9-10). Similarly, God held back the waters of the Red Sea and made a path of deliverance for the people, out of Egypt and away from the fear and barrenness of slavery. So the people beg God to act again and bring them out of their exile in Babylon, back to their own land.

To have some sense of their situation of oppression, it is helpful to think of more recent situations where people experience injustice and are struggling hard for freedom and dignity. What kinds of oppression have you observed in the world? What kinds of oppression do you and your neighbors experience?

- If you were to write an appeal to God, what would you say? Write your own version of this text.

- In verses 12-13, God promises the people that those they fear will fade like grass, and God's creative power is stronger and will last longer than the fury of the oppressor. What do you hear in God's response? What is reassuring? What questions still linger? What would you like to hear back from God?

Closing

Sing or read the hymn, "My Life Flows On," number 580 in *Hymnal: A Worship Book* (Scottdale, Pa: Mennonite Publishing House, 1992), or "Lift Every Voice and Sing," number 579 in *Hymnal: A Worship Book*.

Devotionals

Devotional 1

Look to the rock from which you were hewn, and to the quarry from which you were dug. —Isaiah 51:1b

I don't often think of God as a rock, yet there is something very reassuring about picturing God this way: solid and stable, not easily moved or manipulated. Certainly, when crossing a swift stream and slipping in the muddy soil, it's a welcome relief to step onto a firm rock.

Interestingly, this image for God shows up many times in the Bible. Moses used it five times in his final address to the people of Israel, in Deuteronomy 32. And it is often used in the Psalms, such as Psalm 18:2: "The Lord is my rock, my fortress, and my deliverer, my God, my rock in whom I take refuge."

When life seems out of control, it's good to remember that God's love is secure, a firm foundation on which to stand. It's also comforting to know we were cut out of this Rock and will always belong to God.
–*Linda Gehman Peachey*

Loving God, thank you for being a firm rock on which to rest; help me to trust in your love even when life is confusing and hectic, or too hard to bear.

Devotional 2

Look to Abraham your father and to Sarah who bore you. —Isaiah 51:2a

In my town's newspaper, birth announcements routinely report the parent's names as "Jones, Mr. and Mrs. John M. (Susan Smith)." With her name in parentheses, it's clear the mother is considered a secondary figure, even though she has just done the truly hard work of giving birth.

I find it comforting that even thousands of years ago, Sarah and Abraham were both named in this passage. It's a good reminder of how important it is to recognize everyone involved in an effort. So often our society focuses on those deemed most important or those who play more public roles. But we need to also remember those who do the background tasks, who clean the church, wash the clothes, pick up the trash, and cook the food. How do we make sure these people don't end up in parentheses? How do we give them the honor they deserve? –*Linda Gehman Peachey*

Dear God, help us remember your love for everyone; help us to remember their names.

Devotional 3

He will comfort all her waste places, and will make her wilderness like Eden, her desert like the garden of the Lord. —Isaiah 51:3

What an amazing promise! "God will comfort all her waste places . . ." I admit that I would rather not go there. I try to avoid the waste places, the desolate, gloomy areas where nothing is growing. Both figuratively and literally, it's hard to face the barren spaces of our lives, the places of our world ruined by violence and greed.

Yet, God is not afraid to go there. God doesn't ignore our ruined spaces, but deals with them and brings new life, even in the wilderness. In fact, God seems to specialize in meeting people there. The children of Israel learned much about God's will in their wilderness journey out of Egypt and in their time of exile. John the Baptist spoke to the people from the wilderness and Jesus clarified his mission there. We too need not fear the desert, but can trust God to bring forth abundant life. *–Linda Gehman Peachey*

God of life, walk with us in the wilderness; help us trust your power to bring forth new life even in the waste places.

Devotional 4

My salvation has gone out and my arms will rule the peoples; the coastlands wait for me, and for my arm they hope. —Isaiah 51:5

This really is an audacious claim. From the perspective of Babylon—or any great empire—how can tiny Israel claim that its God will bring salvation to the world? After all, Israel was conquered, its great temple destroyed, its people taken as captives into exile. How dare their God make such grandiose claims?

Years later, Jewish leaders had trouble believing too. When Jesus came to Jerusalem, he wept, saying, "If you . . . had only recognized . . . the things that make for peace! But now they are hidden from your eyes" (Luke 19:41-42).

Amazingly, at Pentecost, people from all over the world did come to believe in this God, and in the way of Jesus. Since then, many more have believed and established communities seeking the salvation God offers. Though the ways of empire are still strong, God's salvation is more powerful, and will bring life and wholeness to the whole world. *–Linda Gehman Peachey*

O strong and loving God, you promised that all peoples will come to you and ask to learn your ways; help us to keep learning and sharing what you teach us.

Devotional 5

Do not fear the reproach of others, and do not be dismayed when they revile you. —Isaiah 51:7b

It's not fun being different. Children know this very early, as they pressure one another to fit in, and tease those who don't belong. And though our culture claims to value individuality, the message of conformity is even louder. Advertisements tell us what we need and what to buy; national holidays and monuments shape who we are and what we can believe.

So we all need to learn that it's okay not to follow the crowd. When a nation pursues war, when women are treated as playthings, when fields and forests are ruined by greed, it's good to pursue a different path.

Of course, it's not healthy to be different just for its own sake. One also needs to belong: to God and to a community of those who seek to follow God's ways. Ultimately, our hope lies in God, whose salvation will outlast all those who mistreat and ridicule others. *–Linda Gehman Peachey*

Dear God, we cringe when others misunderstand us, or we become haughty and judgmental; help us trust you so completely that we can seek the loving way that leads to life.

Devotional 6

The oppressed shall speedily be released; they shall not die . . . nor shall they lack bread.
—Isaiah 51:14

This is a hard promise to believe. Every day, we hear news of people who are still oppressed, still hungry, still dying. How are we to trust this message?

But maybe God is saying something different. Perhaps the main point is that this is not God's will, this is not what God wants. God wants people to be released, to live, to have enough to eat. God is not the one who causes suffering. Rather, the fault lies with those who oppress. But they will not live forever; their power is limited and will be overturned.

It may take many years, but slaves will find freedom, children will go to school and not to the sweatshop, people will find healing from abuse and violence. This is God's desire. This is God's ultimate goal, and we can trust God to help us move toward this promise. *–Linda Gehman Peachey*

O God, it's hard to believe sometimes, that your way of love is stronger than oppression and death; help thou my unbelief.

Devotional 7

I have put my words in your mouth, and hidden you in the shadow of my hand, stretching out the heavens and laying the foundations of the earth. —Isaiah 51:16

This is a fascinating verse. On one hand, God is busy creating the heavens and the earth, while at the same time putting words in the prophet's mouth, and carefully hiding him in the shadow of that creative hand. It's hard to put all the pieces together.

But the implication seems clear. God's creative power is immense and wonderful, but God still needs humans to speak and act. God gives them words to say and cares for their well-being. God doesn't want do this all alone.

This, too, is hard to picture. Why does God need us? Why has God chosen us? It seems that God wants a relationship, a people to work with. God seeks out people to be God's witnesses and represent God's will on earth. It's a humbling, yet astonishing thought, one to ponder and treasure all our days. *–Linda Gehman Peachey*

Dear God, we marvel at your creation, but even more we are amazed you seek us out and trust us with your words; help us rest in the shadow of your love and seek to follow your ways.

Finding satisfaction

Isaiah 55:1-11

Opening

Recall a time when you felt especially thirsty—either physically or spiritually. What quenched your thirst? Did you try anything that left you even thirstier than before?

Understanding the Word

Throughout chapters 40–55, the prophet has conveyed God's pardon and God's intention for Israel. Not only would they survive their time in exile, but they were to be a light to all nations. Isaiah 55 summons the community to accept the almost unbelievable news that God was once more to be their God.

The invitation to those who thirst and hunger sums up this message of comfort. Kings often celebrated the inauguration of their reign by throwing a great banquet, so the invitation to come and drink and eat is really an announcement of the restoration of God's kingdom with Israel. Life, history, and their existence suddenly is to have meaning again. Although now living in the poverty of exile, they could buy "without money and without cost." Their king, a gracious God, is picking up the tab.

Now that God has spoken, Israel is summoned to respond. Respond now! If it seems that over the 50 years of exile God's face has been hidden,

For the leader

1. Bring a pitcher of refreshing water and enough cups for everyone in the group. After a time of sharing around the circle, enjoy the water together.

2. Ask everyone to read the passage through silently, and then listen as someone reads it dramatically. What words or phrases stand out in this text? What is God saying to you?

now God is near, now God invites all to the banquet of restoration. Yes, there are many in Israel who have been "wicked." The invitation is extended to the wicked as well as the virtuous. If the wicked demonstrate repentance by forsaking their evil actions and thoughts, God's mercy is assured. God will "freely pardon."

Connecting with God's Word

Finding that which satisfies

How is it that a word of God to Israel in exile so quickly becomes a word of God to us? One reason may be that there is exile in all of us. We are estranged from our best selves, our most meaningful lives. Especially in North America, we settle for that which we can buy with money, for that which can never really satisfy. We can buy a certain illusion of independence, but that very independence cuts us off from a richer fabric of relationships and interdependence.

In Barbara Kingsolver's novel *The Bean Trees* (New York: HarperCollins, 1988), one of the characters, an illegal immigrant from Guatemala, tells a story of "how they eat in hell." There is plenty of food on the table in hell, he explains, but the damned are given only very long spoons with which to eat it. With these spoons they cannot get the food to their mouths, and they curse and starve and suffer.

He then tells "how they eat in heaven." In heaven there are the same tables, the same food, and the same long spoons. There, however, they eat like this—and he takes some food on his spoon and reaches across the table to the child across from him, who opens her mouth and takes it in. Feeding each other, those in heaven partake of an endless, plentiful, and joyful banquet.

A consumer culture offers options and, for many, a high level of purchasing power. Why is it that, in general, such a culture fails to provide real satisfaction? To what extent is it true that "The more I eat, the hungrier I get"?

In John 7:37 Jesus, apparently echoing Isaiah 55:1, stands and calls out, "If anyone is thirsty, let him come to me and drink."

- How does someone know he or she is "thirsty"? What are the symptoms of thirst Jesus refers to here? Who is *not* thirsty?

- Who is "anyone"? Are there any limitations on those to whom this invitation is extended? When your congregation invites others, do they perceive any unspoken limitations on your invitation, based on what they see and hear from you?

- How does one "come to" Jesus? Does your congregation have a clear, common understanding about how one comes to Jesus and "drinks"?

My ways are not your ways

God's plans and purposes, even the readiness of God's mercy, may seem beyond comprehension. They are. That's part of the good news. Despair comes from the inevitable failure of human efforts to grasp divine purpose and measure divine mercy. They are, thank God, beyond our calculations and estimates.

God also promises that "my word will not return to me empty." Behind this poetic metaphor is the subtle reminder that it is God who has created and sustains the earth. It is God who sends rain and snow to water the earth, making it generative and fertile. Just as the rain enters the earth, and just as its effects may be hidden there for a time before it bears fruit, so the word of the Lord may be submerged and silent for a time, but inevitably it achieves the purpose for which God sent it (v. 11).

The dormant period of God's word and purpose is coming to a close. Israel's faith, tested by long exile, may fail. God's word will not. And that word, right before their disbelieving eyes, is about to bear fruit.

- What experiences in your life illustrate that God's thoughts and purposes are beyond ours—that our expectations and predictions of God's will and action are frustrated by our inadequate understanding?

- When have you experienced the truth that God's word is fulfilled, that God's way did come to fulfillment?

- How does faith in God's ultimate success affect your daily life? How does this influence what you do and the decisions you make?

Closing

Sing or listen to the hymn, "O Let All Who Thirst," number 495 in *Hymnal: A Worship Book* (Scottdale, Pa: Mennonite Publishing House, 1992). Pray for the wisdom and courage to "come to the Lord."

Devotionals

Devotional 1

Ho, everyone who thirsts, come to the waters; and you that have no money, come, buy and eat! —Isaiah 55:1

Like many North Americans, my greatest hungers and thirsts are not for food and drink but for time. How I yearn for a few extra hours each day to get things done—or even to do nothing at all!

As a seminary student with many assignments to complete, I was often tempted to skip my devotional time. I soon came to realize the truth of Martin Luther's observation that I was "too busy not to pray." I was spending time on "that which does not satisfy" (v. 2). When I neglected my devotional life, it took longer to get things done because I was more distracted and frustrated by the challenges of the day.

Today as you look to the things that need to be done and deadlines to meet, listen to God's invitation to "incline your ear, and come to me; listen, so that you may live" (v. 3). *–Matt Hamsher*

God, you know the challenges that face me today. Help me center my thoughts upon you so that I can receive your peace and guidance in every moment.

Devotional 2

Eat what is good, and delight yourselves in rich food. —Isaiah 55:2

In the movie *Babette's Feast*, the best cook in Paris escapes the French Revolution and finds sanctuary with two dour Christian sisters. When Babette wins the lottery, she wants to prepare a meal for her hosts and their friends. The sisters reluctantly agree, but the guests agree not to compliment the cook or enjoy themselves too much.

Course after course of delectable dishes arrive at the table, and the meal slowly melts the hard hearts of the guests. Several quarreling members reconcile, and they end the evening singing and dancing together. They have been transformed by Babette's feast of love.

Isaiah 55 is a delightful invitation to a celebration at God's table. The images of flowing waters, milk, wine, and rich foods may seem too abundant. We may not think we deserve such generosity. May God's meal of love melt our hearts so we may extend God's grace to those around us. *–Patty Friesen*

Who is a pard'ning God like thee? Or who has grace so rich and free, or who has grace so rich and free? —Samuel Davies

Devotional 3

Incline your ear, and come to me; listen so that you may live. I will make with you an everlasting covenant, my steadfast, sure love. —Isaiah 55:3

Last night, Mariya had to interview her family for a school report: our favorite possessions, candy, and so on. The question I had to think about longest was "What's your favorite holiday?" I thought about how this answer has changed over the years. It's been my birthday, Christmas, and Mother's Day, but last night I told Mariya it was her birthday.

Mariya's birthday is a wonderful reminder of the decision I made, years ago, to love this girl. I didn't wait to find out all the implications of that decision. I don't decide each day on the basis of what she does or doesn't do, whether or not I love her.

She's the one who most helps me understand this Scripture. God committed to loving me and each of us, long before we were born. I'm sure God has many favorite holidays, and I'm happy to know my birthday is one of them!
—*Sandra Drescher Lehman*

Thank you, Lord, for your everlasting covenant of love that envelops me and gives me the examples I need.

Devotional 4

See, you shall call nations that you do not know, and nations that you do not know shall run to you. —Isaiah 55:5

Modern statecraft is nothing if not calculated. Leaders of nations huddle with advisers to gather information and consider every outcome before making decisions. On a personal level we also like to orchestrate outcomes.

Isaiah 55 calls the Israelites to use their covenant with God, rather than human perspectives, in order to find abundant life. Instead of trying to control the future, they are to lead a life that attracts others and to let God furnish the details.

The result is we become open to opportunities and relationships we did not know existed. A previously unknown neighbor becomes a trusted friend. Radical hospitality and openness to all people is the place in which God works.

Try as we might to understand, verse 9 concludes that we can't: "For as the heavens are higher than the earth, so are my ways higher than your ways, and my thoughts than your thoughts." —*Brent Hershey*

Today, Lord, help me recognize and release my self-serving strategies and efforts; teach me to practice a hospitality that serves your ways.

Devotional 5

*Nations that do not know you shall run to you, because of the L*ORD *your God . . . for he has glorified you. —Isaiah 55:5*

This passage begins in the marketplace. Sellers are hawking their wares, vying for the attention of choosy shoppers. But something is different. "Why pay when you can eat and drink for free?"

Why indeed? Our large family always had enough to eat, but there weren't always second helpings. A company picnic I attended when I was young is especially memorable. Everything was free and you could eat as much as you wanted. At that picnic I ate huge mounds of hamburgers, hot dogs, and ice cream.

I wonder if that glorious day inspired my wife and me in our annual fiesta. For many years we've fed our congregation and their guests. We're happiest when we see people we've never met. They're our most welcome guests.

We hope they see a model of God's limitless and unconditional love. God calls all of us, including nations we do not know, to a feast of love. —*Frank Ramirez*

God, thank you for inviting all who seek to come to the water, and all who have nothing, to come to you.

Devotional 6

As the rain and snow . . . yields seed for the sower and bread for the eater, so is my word that goes out from my mouth.
—Isaiah 55:10-11 (NIV)

As I write, the Bing cherry tree in my backyard is nearing the end of its fruit season. I tried to pick all the cherries I possibly could. I also gave away many so there would be fewer going to waste.

I find myself savoring the last few cherries of the season and trying to commit the taste to memory. Of course, there will be the frozen cherries stored away in the freezer, but their flavor does not come close to that of the fresh fruit.

This passage reminds us that the bounties of our earth such as seed, bread—and cherries—come to us because of rain and snow sent by God. Further, through wonderful word pictures, describing mountains and hills bursting into song and trees of the field clapping their hands (v. 12), we also recognize that God's creation already acknowledges what we are still learning: that God's word will be accomplished.
–Robert Hoffman

God, your ways are higher than our ways. Please make your thoughts our thoughts today.

Devotional 7

So shall my word be that goes out from my mouth; it shall not return to me empty, but it shall accomplish that which I purpose.
—Isaiah 55:11

My friend, a second grade teacher, knows that repetition is key to training her students in the way they should go. But she gets tired of repeating herself. And it's a good thing I'm not a teacher. I want people to hear me the first time.

Not only that, I want my words to return full of accomplished tasks. When I send someone to get the mail, I want the mail to appear on my table. When I send someone to make the bed upstairs, I want to see the bed made. I want results.

Isaiah 55 is stuffed with examples of how God's words come back full of promise. There are delicious gifts (bread, wine, and milk vv. 1-2), a God much bigger than we are (v. 9) and a happy earth (v. 12). So why should I not believe that the good words God speaks will accomplish what God desires? –Lani Wright

Dear God, let me claim the promises of milk not bought with money, of results not simply dependent on my labor. Let me buy into what is good.

Good news

Isaiah 61

Opening

This passage opens with God sending a wonderful message to people in need of deliverance and healing. Who in your community or nation needs such a message? Who is bringing that good news?

Understanding God's Word

The words in this text were likely addressed to Jewish exiles who had returned to Judah, and were finding resettlement difficult. Ivan Friesen writes that "Those who hear this good news are probably repatriated exiles from Babylon, seeking to break free from their poverty and discouragement" (*Isaiah*, Believers Church Bible Commentary, Scottdale, Pa: Herald Press, 2009, 395). No doubt, life there was more daunting than they had anticipated, not at all as they had imagined it would be.

For the leader

1. Read or sing together "Holy Spirit, Come with Power," number 26 in *Hymnal: A Worship Book* (Scottdale, Pa: Mennonite Publishing House, 1992).

2. Point out that the beginning of this chapter is an important text for Christians, as Jesus used it as a basis for his ministry. To understand this more fully, ask one person to read Isaiah 11:1-3 and another to read Luke 4:14-19. What words or ideas are similar? What is different?

3. Note that in Matthew 11:2-5, when John's disciples came to Jesus asking whether he is the "one who is to come," Jesus responded by highlighting these signs: "The blind receive their sight, the lame walk, the lepers are cleansed, the deaf hear, the dead are raised, and the poor have good news brought to them."

There are many promises in Isaiah 61:

- a promise of healing, liberty, and release from debt (vv. 1-2)
- a promise of gladness and praise rather than mourning and weakness (v. 3)
- a promise of restoration and honor among the nations (vv. 4-7)
- a promise of a renewed covenant (vv. 8-9)

The chapter concludes with a response of joy and praise, with the prophet trusting that just as the earth brings forth new growth, so too God will bring forth righteousness among the nations.

Connecting with God's Word

Anointed with God's spirit

In this passage, the messenger of salvation is likely the prophet himself. But before he explains his mission, he speaks of being authorized and equipped: "The spirit of the Lord God is upon me . . . the Lord has anointed me."

The Bible speaks often of God's spirit being given to prophets and other leaders, as blessing and empowerment to do God's work (Isaiah 11:2-5, 42:1; Ezekiel 11:5; Micah 3:8; Matthew 3:16). References to God's spirit also connect back to creation, when God's spirit moved over the waters and breathed life into human beings.

No doubt, people would have heard this as a message of hope, a sign that God was moving among the people and creating newness and life out of the wilderness of their existence.

- How do you understand being "anointed with God's Spirit"? How does your congregation understand the Spirit's role in sharing God's good news?

"The year of the Lord's favor"

This message of hope is addressed to several needy groups: the poor, the brokenhearted, captives, prisoners, and those who mourn. They are then addressed precisely with what is appropriate to their need: good news, binding up, freedom, release, comfort, and the year of the Lord's favor.

This last phrase refers to the year of Jubilee outlined in Leviticus 25, when the land was to rest, property given back to the original owner, and those who had been sold into slavery were to be set free. Ivan Friesen writes that central to the proclamation is "the notion of liberty for Israelites who have experienced loss of land and other economic hardship." Further, in both Leviticus and Isaiah 61, "there is an emphasis . . . on a general amnesty for the impoverished and downtrodden" (*Isaiah*, Believers Church Bible Commentary,

Scottdale, Pa: Herald Press, 2009, 395). The salvation God offers is holistic; it addresses spiritual, psychological, physical, and economic needs.

Many have noticed that when Jesus read this passage in Luke 4:18-19, he did not include the rest of verse 2: "the day of vengeance of our God." No doubt this was deliberate, as Jesus emphasized loving all people, even one's enemies. He made this even more clear in his comments after the reading, when he noted how God helped the widow from Sidon and Naaman the Syrian. In this way, Jesus opened up the hope of Jubilee to all people, Jews and Gentiles.

Even in Isaiah, though, the text does not dwell on vengeance. Rather, the passage moves quickly to promise comfort for those who mourn. Clearly, this is the more important theme, as three sets of contrasting images are given: a garland rather than ashes, oil of gladness rather than mourning, a mantle of praise rather than a faint spirit.

- What would the year of Jubilee look like in your context? Who needs this message?
- Who in your community is working to bring liberty and healing to the poor and brokenhearted? How are you involved in these efforts?

Rejoicing in God

The chapter ends with a wonderful hymn of praise. The prophet seems to relax in gratitude and trust in God. There are images of a wedding and being dressed for a banquet, both lavish, joyful occasions. Finally, there is the wonderful image of the earth at springtime, bringing forth new life and sustenance.

- When do you feel most thankful? How do you express gratitude and praise?
- How does your congregation nurture and express thankfulness and praise?
- How do you explain the intersection between joy and ministry? Discuss the following quotations: Archbishop William Temple says, "True joy happens when *what one must do* converges with *what one most wants to do*." Author Frederick Buechner says, "The place God calls you is the place where your deep gladness and the world's deep hunger meet." (Quotations from Walter Brueggemann, *The Covenanted Self: Explorations in Law and Covenant*, Minneapolis, MN: Fortress, 1999, 33.)

Closing

Read Isaiah 61:10-11 together as a joyful affirmation of faith.

Devotionals

Devotional 1

The spirit of the Lord God . . . has anointed me; he has sent me to bring good news to the oppressed. —Isaiah 61:1

This chapter leaves me awestruck. As Christians we have been anointed by the Holy Spirit to spread the gospel, minister to broken and hurting people, and free those held captive by evil.

If the chapter ended here, this would be a large task, but there is actually more! God could call on us to deliver a message of conviction and call to repentance (v. 2). We are also to comfort those in mourning, and bring gladness back to their lives (vv. 2-3).

These verses paint a beautiful picture of the ideal Christian community. Imagine every person responding in love to the vulnerabilities we all have. We could help each other repair ruined lives and heal broken hearts. We could extend God's love beyond ourselves to a hurting world. Supporting each other as the Holy Spirit intends, we would be like a healthy oak tree standing firm in a chaotic world. *–Helen Balzer*

Today, Lord, when I feel your nudge to do some good in the world, help me to respond in obedience.

Devotional 2

The spirit of the Lord God . . . has sent me to bring good news to the oppressed, to bind up the brokenhearted, to proclaim liberty to the captives. —Isaiah 61:1

Riding the bus or pausing at crowded street corners in my city, I see plenty of the people described in Isaiah 61. The weary dad with a toddler may be seeking release. The young woman–dreadfully thin and exquisitely dressed–may be captive to fashion standards. The woman with the cane struggling onto the bus appears faint of spirit.

Christians remember that Jesus did all these things in his Spirit-appointed ministry. He brought good news to the oppressed, bound up the brokenhearted, and proclaimed liberty to the captives. If we are attentive, we find ourselves in this good news, and bear witness to how Jesus saves and heals us.

There's also a nudge in these verses. As Jesus-followers, we too are appointed to continue the ministry. Whether in teeming cities or quiet villages, we are invited to proclaim God's good news–to bind up the brokenhearted, comfort the mourners, and work for justice. *–Melissa Miller*

Liberating God, friend of the captive and the brokenhearted, guide us to use our hands and feet, our voices and hearts to proclaim your good news.

Devotional 3

The spirit of the Lord God . . . has sent me to bring good news to the oppressed, to bind up the brokenhearted. —Isaiah 61:1

One morning, I found a note on my desk. "We love you," it read. That message from my colleagues gave me energy for a busy day. It also reminded me of the power of words. How often has someone either made or broken our day with a single remark?

When our sons were teenagers, we had to work especially hard at communication. The boys were going and coming to school and work, and we parents worked in different locations. So we developed a system of writing notes, which often brought us smiles.

God also comes to us with words that renew body and spirit. Isaiah proclaimed good news to the oppressed. These words would have energized the discouraged people of Israel as they languished in exile in Babylon. They continue to give us hope, as we see this good news proclaimed again by Jesus (Luke 4) and by his followers today. *–Bertha Toews Born*

Lord, we thank you for the good news that you love us. Help us to encourage others by well-placed words of cheer when we have a chance.

Devotional 4

The spirit of the Lord God is upon me, because the Lord has anointed me . . . to proclaim the year of the Lord's favor. —Isaiah. 61:1a, 2a.

In Israel, God ordained that every seventh day and seventh year would be a Sabbath, when people and the land could rest. Furthermore, every seventh Sabbath year would be a "year of Jubilee." That year, all slaves would be freed, those forced by poverty to sell their lands would receive them back, and those in prison released.

This is what Jesus proclaimed when he read Isaiah 61 in the synagogue (Luke 4:16-21). He came to bring good news to the poor, bind up the brokenhearted, free slaves, open doors of darkness, untie people's hands, unfold their wings! He came to proclaim the year of God's grace, of Jubilee!

But it was not just once every 50 years. Jesus came to bring a worldwide Jubilee that every year, every day, would speak good news to the poor, liberty to captives, healing to the broken. This is what God wants for you, and everyone! *–Bob Hostetler*

Lord, thank you for your deliverance; please make this year a Jubilee in my life and help me share Jubilee with those around me.

Devotional 5

They shall build up . . . raise up . . . repair . . . the devastations of many generations. —Isaiah 61:4

At bedtime I call, "Kids, clean up, please!" Often, I need to repeat my instructions. Eventually, my children pick up every block, toy, or animal.

I wonder what Isaiah felt when he proclaimed, "The Lord has sent me to bring good news, liberty, release, favor, comfort, gladness, praise" (vv. 1-3a). Years of selfish behavior had brought ruin, a huge mess to their life as a nation. Did Isaiah believe these positive outcomes would occur in his lifetime?

Do I trust God to work restoration in seemingly hopeless situations? How do any of us embrace the immediacy of this good news?

It helps to pick up the pieces one at a time—to act upon the command that is also a promise, to keep bringing good news to people in faith. *–Doug Schulz*

Lord, build in me a hopeful spirit. Today let me lift up myself and others with confidence that you will still bring your promises to fulfillment in our lives.

Devotional 6

All who see them shall acknowledge that they are a people whom the Lord *has blessed. —Isaiah 61:9*

When Jesus announced the beginning of his ministry, he picked this text (Luke 4:16-19). It also introduces Jesus as a king, doing things only a king can do. Only a king can bring good news to the oppressed, bind the brokenhearted, release prisoners and captives, and comfort all who mourn.

What joy to be subjects of a king like this! With a ruler who cares for the people like this, those watching would acknowledge that these are people whom God has blessed.

We must not forget however, that our King loves justice, hates wrongdoing, and brings to account those who practice injustice or the abuse of others. We cannot receive the joy of the King without also understanding how he wants us to live.

Someone wrote, "I don't care how high you jump when you praise the Lord. Just make certain you are walking straight when your feet hit the ground." *–Jim Holm*

Lord, I'm so glad you are sovereign and will someday rule the world. As your subject, help me practice your justice and right living today.

Devotional 7

I will greatly rejoice in the Lord *. . . for he has clothed me with the garments of salvation. —Isaiah 61:10*

In this chapter, Isaiah uses beautiful word pictures to describe God's work. The prophet speaks of a crown of beauty, a garment of praise, garments of salvation, a robe of righteousness, a bridegroom adorning his head, and a bride adorning herself with jewels.

In the first verse, however, Isaiah refers to anointing. In his time, this meant applying an aromatic ointment—often expensive—to the entire body. It was considered a luxury, and thus not done during periods of mourning.

At first I resisted this picture. Perhaps it's because I belong to a culture that tries to wash away all traces of oil or scent from one's body and clothes. Even more difficult was the thought of wearing festive adornment while binding up wounds and freeing prisoners.

As I reread Isaiah's words, however, I see a wonderful new vision: work for God that the Spirit transforms into acts of celebration. *–Janet Toews Berg*

Holy Spirit, because you have anointed me, today is more than just an ordinary day. It is a day of celebration of the good news of Jesus.

CPSIA information can be obtained at www.ICGtesting.com
Printed in the USA
BVOW081341190712

295607BV00007B/22/P